Simple Machines

Pulleys

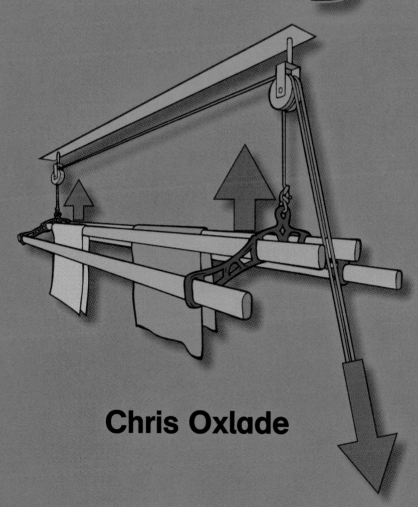

Chris Oxlade

W

FRANKLIN WATTS

LONDON•SYDNEY

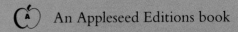 An Appleseed Editions book

First published in 2007 by Franklin Watts

Franklin Watts
338 Euston Road, London NW1 3BH

Franklin Watts Australia
Hachette Children's Books
Level 17/207 Kent St, Sydney, NSW 2000

© 2007 Appleseed Editions

Created by Appleseed Editions Ltd, Well House,
Friars Hill, Guestling, East Sussex TN35 4ET

Designed by Helen James
Edited by Mary-Jane Wilkins
Artwork by Bill Donohoe

ISBN 978 0 7496 7567 7

Dewey Classification: 621.8' 62

A CIP catalogue for this book is available from the British Library

Photo credits
Page 5 Richard Cummins/Corbis; 6 Rick Ergenbright/Corbis; 9 Neil Rabinowitz/
Corbis; 11 Michael S. Yamashita/Corbis; 12 Adam Woolfitt/Corbis; 14 Chris Oxlade;
17 Galen Rowell/Corbis; 18 Adrian Wilson/Beateworks/Corbis; 19 James L. Amos/
Corbis; 20 Car Culture/Corbis; 21 Chris Oxlade; 22 Studio Wartenberg/Zefa/Corbis;
23 Negri, Brescia/Corbis; 26 Chris Oxlade; 28 courtesey Carey & Fox Ltd; 29t Phil
Schermeister/Corbis, b Chris Oxlade

Printed in China

Franklin Watts is a division of Hachette Children's Books

Contents

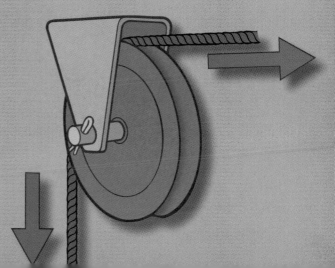

What is a simple machine?

A simple machine is something that helps you to do a job. We use simple machines to help us every day. Here are some simple machines you might find at home or school.

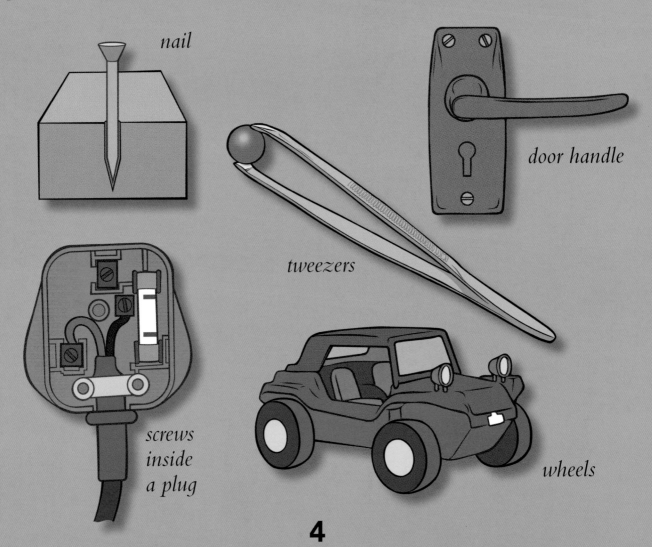

nail

door handle

tweezers

screws inside a plug

wheels

This book is about simple machines called pulleys. Pulleys help us to lift and move things.

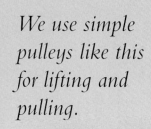

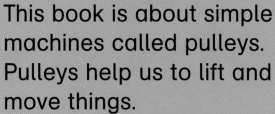

An old iron pulley on a farmyard water well.

We use simple pulleys like this for lifting and pulling.

Pushes and pulls

You pull on a pulley's rope to make the pulley work. When you pull, the pulley makes a pull too. Scientists call pulls like this forces. They call pushes forces, too.

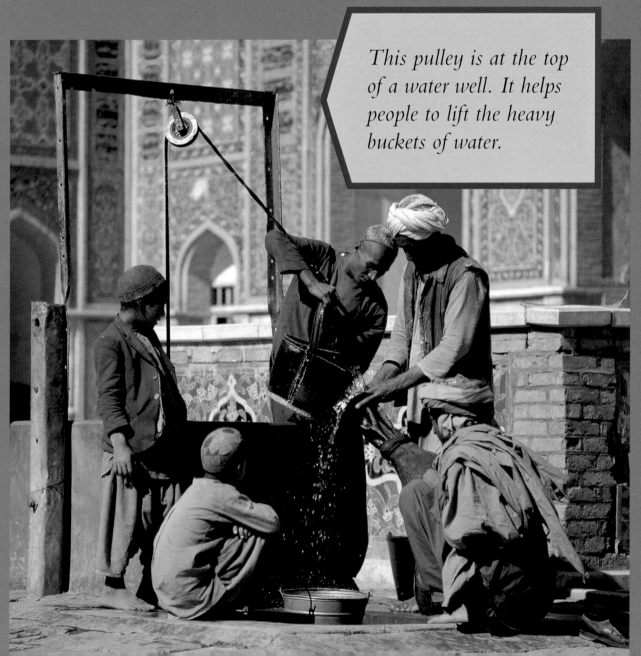

This pulley is at the top of a water well. It helps people to lift the heavy buckets of water.

We show forces with arrows. The arrow points in the direction that the force is pushing or pulling. The longer the arrow, the bigger the pull or push is.

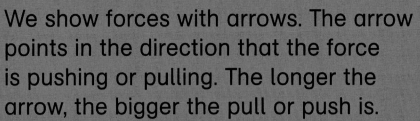

This force arrow shows that the child's weight is pushing down on the chair.

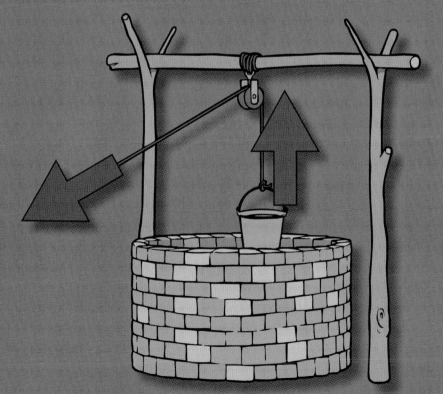

The person pulls down on the rope. The rope pulls up on the bucket.

Red arrows show pushes and pulls.

Blue arrows show movement.

How a pulley works

A simple pulley is made up of a pulley wheel and a rope.

The pulley wheel has a groove around the outside. The rope fits into the groove. The wheel spins round on its axle.

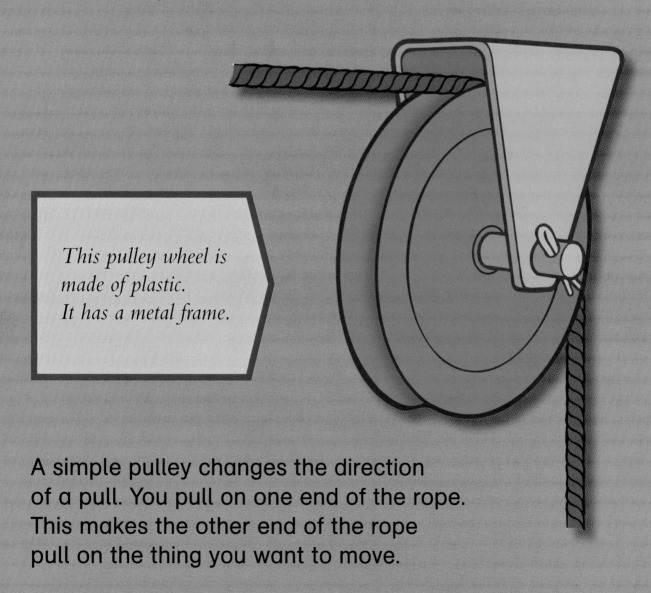

This pulley wheel is made of plastic. It has a metal frame.

A simple pulley changes the direction of a pull. You pull on one end of the rope. This makes the other end of the rope pull on the thing you want to move.

These sailors are pulling on ropes to raise sails on a boat. The ropes go over pulleys at the top of the mast.

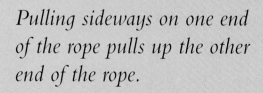

Pulling sideways on one end of the rope pulls up the other end of the rope.

How pulleys work together

Pulleys often work together. We can put a rope around two pulleys. Pulling on the rope makes the pulleys move towards each other.

This sort of pulley is called a block and tackle.

We can use two pulleys to lift a heavy weight. The pulleys make it easier to lift things so a light pull can lift a heavy load.

Fishermen use a block and tackle to lift heavy fishing nets on to their boat.

A small pull on the rope makes a larger pull on the hook.

11

Lifting with simple pulleys

Most pulleys are used to lift heavy loads.

A simple pulley makes lifting easier because you can use your weight to help pull down on the rope. Builders lift building materials with simple pulleys.

A pulley lifting a heavy bucket to the upper floors of a house.

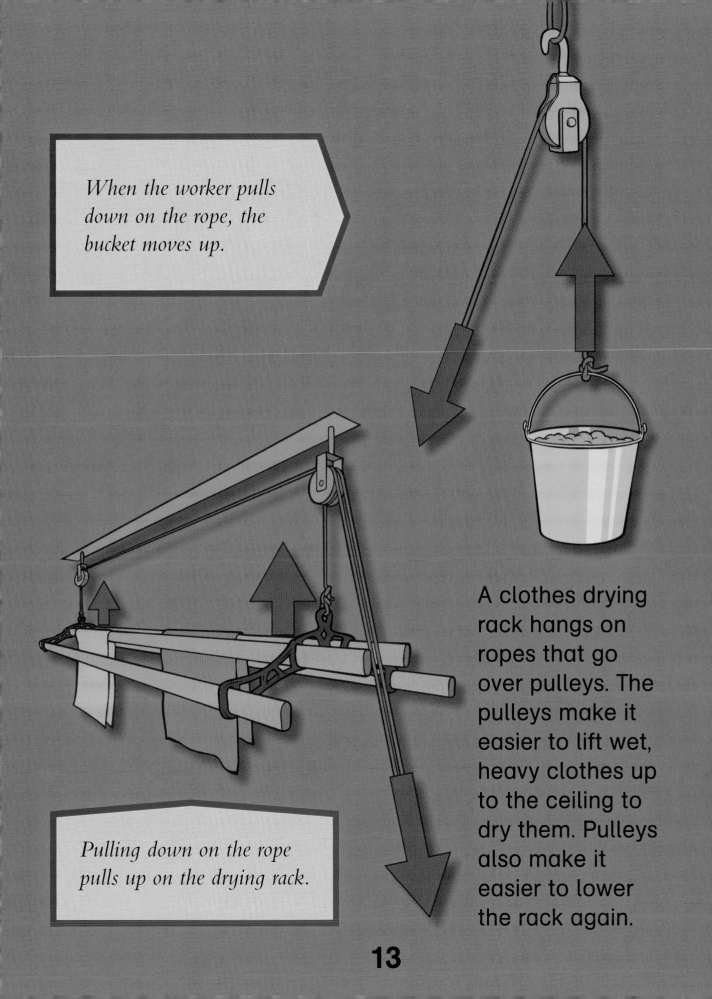

When the worker pulls down on the rope, the bucket moves up.

Pulling down on the rope pulls up on the drying rack.

A clothes drying rack hangs on ropes that go over pulleys. The pulleys make it easier to lift wet, heavy clothes up to the ceiling to dry them. Pulleys also make it easier to lower the rack again.

Heavy lifting with pulleys

We use a block and tackle when we need to lift very heavy loads.

A block and tackle makes lifting much easier. Lifeboats on ships are lifted and lowered by pulleys.

There is a block and tackle at both ends of this boat.

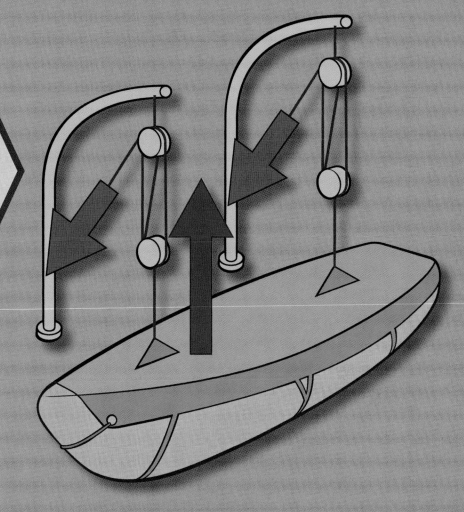

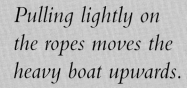

Pulling lightly on the ropes moves the heavy boat upwards.

Some pulleys have metal chains instead of ropes. Mechanics use block and tackles with chains to lift engines from cars and boats to mend them.

A chain hoist. Pulling on the chain loop makes the hook move up or down.

Moving with pulleys

We use pulleys to move things as well as to lift them up.

Pulleys are useful for moving things that are out of reach. In large buildings, pulleys open windows and curtains.

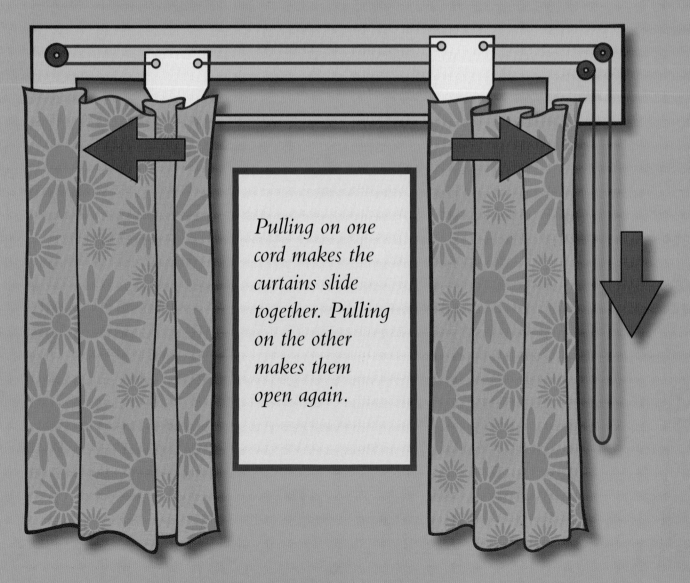

Pulling on one cord makes the curtains slide together. Pulling on the other makes them open again.

Rescue workers sometimes use pulleys. When a heavy truck overturns, mechanics may need to use pulleys to pull it upright again.

Rescuers are using a chain pulley to tip an overturned truck back on to its wheels.

A recovery truck holds one end of a wire and pulls the other end with a winch.

Pulleys in machines

Complicated machines often use pulleys to work.

Some exercise machines in gyms have lots of pulleys. Pulling on one end of the wire lifts a heavy weight. Making the pull is good exercise.

Where are the pulleys on these exercise machines?

Sailing dinghies have lots of pulleys. They help a sailor to pull on a dinghy's sails. This would be difficult without the pulleys.

These pulleys help to change the position of the boat's sail.

Construction cranes use pulleys. A pulley lets a crane lift very heavy loads. The crane's hook is attached to the pulley block. The crane's engine pulls the wire to raise the hook.

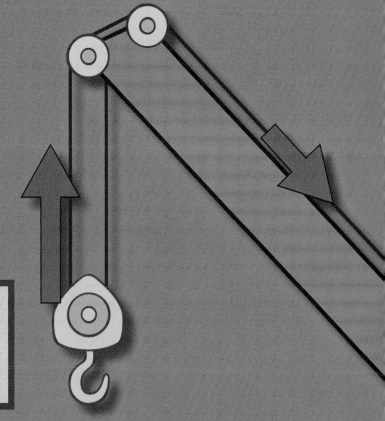

This is the pulley block on a mobile crane.

Pulley wheels

Pulleys are often used to make one wheel turn another wheel.

There are pulley wheels in a car engine.
A rubber belt goes around them all.
The engine turns one of the wheels.
This makes all the other wheels turn, too.

The fan belt in an engine turns pulley wheels. The wheels make parts of the engine work.

A washing machine has pulley wheels. There is one on the electric motor and one on the drum that holds the washing. A rubber belt goes round the wheels.

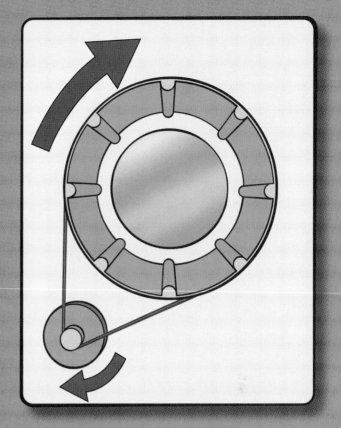

The pulley wheels in a washing machine let the motor turn the drum.

A bicycle has pulley wheels too. There is one on the pedals and one on the back wheel. These pulley wheels have teeth on them.

The pulleys are joined by a metal chain.

Pulleys in the past

People have been using pulleys for thousands of years.

The ancient Romans and ancient Greeks used pulleys to lift building materials and to unload boats.

Sailing ships used many pulleys. Sailors used the pulleys to lift sails up masts and to control the sails.

Pulley wheels on an old sailing ship.

These pulleys worked machines called looms that made cloth.

Pulley wheels were used in factories. A steam engine or water wheel made some pulley wheels turn. Belts from these wheels worked the factory machines.

In medieval times, builders used pulleys to lift materials.

Pulley fun

On the next four pages are some activities for you to do. They will help you to understand how pulleys work.

A SIMPLE PULLEY

You will need:
• two old CDs
• a cardboard tube (such as the centre of a kitchen paper roll)
• a pencil
• string
• sticky tape and scissors

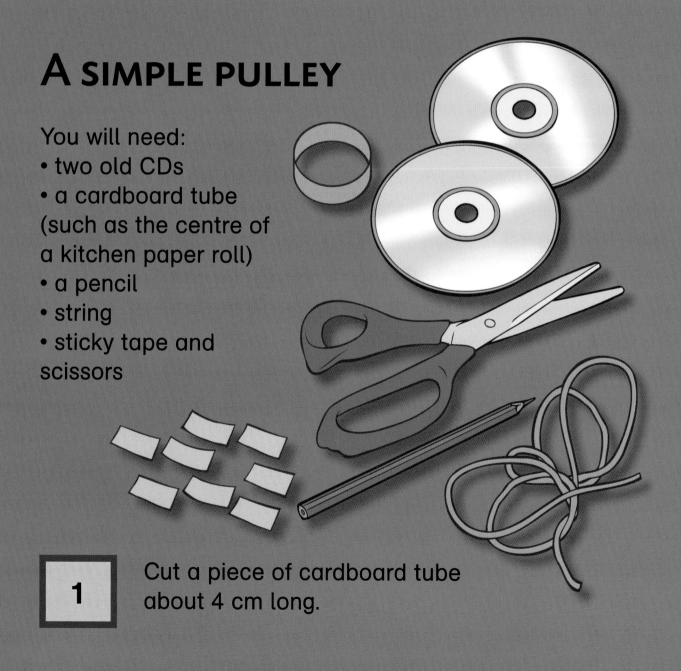

1 Cut a piece of cardboard tube about 4 cm long.

2 Fix the tube to the centre of a CD with sticky tape.

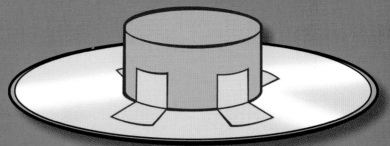

3 Tape another CD on the other end of the tube.

4 Put a pencil through the holes in the CDs. This is a pulley wheel.

5 Tie an object (such as a plastic cup) to a piece of string

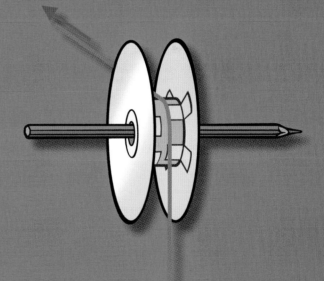

6 Put the string over the pulley wheel and pull to lift the object.

The pulley changes the direction of your pull.

A BLOCK AND TACKLE

You can see how a block and tackle
works using paper clips for pulleys.

You will need:
• two large paper clips
• string

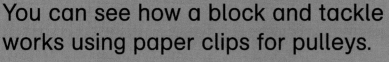

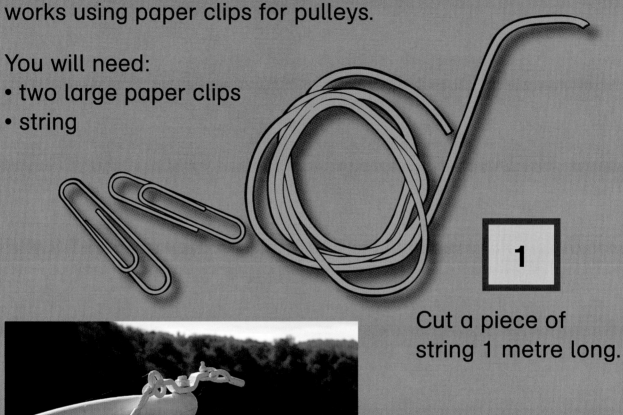

1

Cut a piece of
string 1 metre long.

*This block and tackle is
used to lift a boat on to
the deck of a ship.*

2 Look at a paper clip. One end has two metal loops. Tie one end of the string to the end loop.

3 Loop the string through the end of another paper clip.

4 Now loop the string through the second loop in the first paper clip.

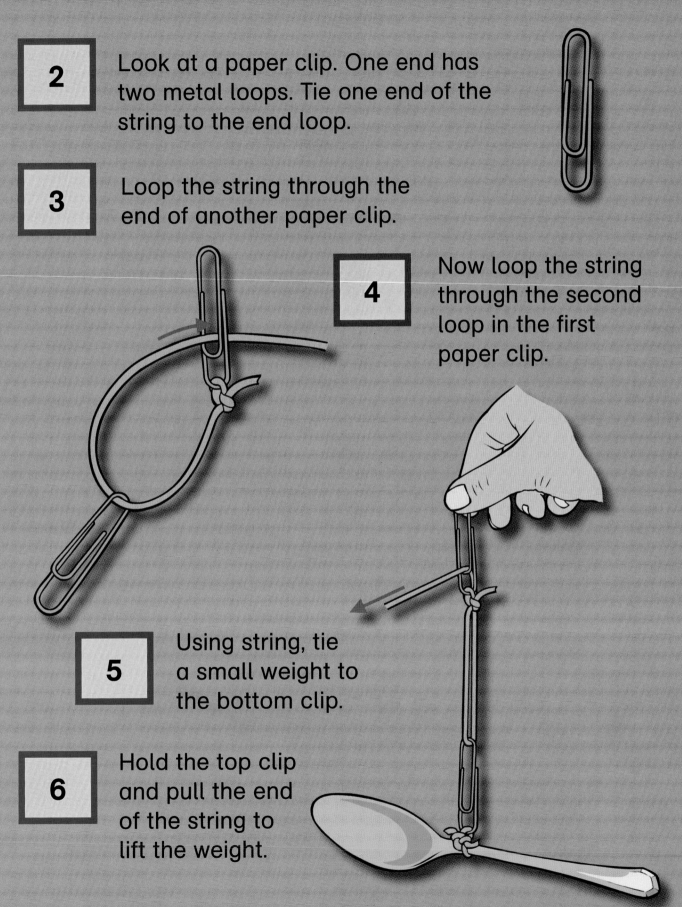

5 Using string, tie a small weight to the bottom clip.

6 Hold the top clip and pull the end of the string to lift the weight.

Spot the pulley

Can you spot all the pulleys
on these pages? Try to work out
what each pulley does.

Where is the pulley here?
What does it help to lift?

Can you see the pulley wheels here? What are they doing?

These are overhead cables on a railway. Where is the pulley?

Answers are on page 32.

Words to remember

axle
A rod joined to the centre of a pulley wheel.
An axle lets the wheel turn easily.

block and tackle
A machine which has two or more pulley
wheels with a wire or rope going around them.
A block and tackle makes a pull on a rope
much larger.

crane
A machine that lifts very heavy loads.
Cranes use pulleys to work.

dinghy
A small boat which is moved along by oars
or a sail.

exercise machine
A machine worked by a person pushing or pulling
on its handles. Working the machine is good exercise.

fan belt
Part of a car's engine, like a long, thick elastic band.

forces
Pushes or pulls.

lifeboat
A boat on a ship which the crew and passengers climb into if the ship begins to sink.

mechanic
Someone who mends machines.

pulley block
A block of material with one or more pulley wheels inside. Two pulley blocks are needed to make a block and tackle.

well
A deep hole in the ground which people take water from.

Index

Answers to pages 28-29

The pulley is part of a window. It helps to lift the bottom window upwards when the window is opened.

These pulley wheels are part of a ski lift. The cable that carries the ski chairs goes over the pulley wheels.

You can see three pulley wheels in a block and tackle.

They let the weight beside the pole pull the cables tight.